Sophocles'

ANTIGONE

•

Adapted by

BERTOLT BRECHT

•

Based on the German Translation by
Friedrich Hölderlin

•

and Translated into English by
JUDITH MALINA

THEATRE BOOK PUBLISHERS

An Applause Original

Sophocles' ANTIGONE in a version by Bertolt Brecht,
translated by Judith Malina

Library of Congress Cataloging-in-Publication Data

Brecht, Bertolt, 1898-1956.
  Sophocles' Antigone / adapted by Bertolt Brecht ;
translated by Judith Malina.
     p.   cm.
  ISBN 0-936839-25-2
   I. Antigone (Lengendary character)—drama. I. Sophocles. Antigone. II. Title.
PT2603.R397S67   1990
832'.912—dc20   90–42
                                                                           CIP

First Applause printing, 1990

Applause Theatre & Cinema Books
19 West 21ST Street, Suite 201
New York, NY 10010
Phone: (212) 575-9265
Fax: (212) 575-9270
Email: info@applausepub.com
Internet: www.applausepub.com

Applause books are available through your local bookstore, or you may order at
www.applausepub.com or call Music Dispatch at 800-637-2852

Sales & Distribution:
North America:
  Hal Leonard Corp.
  7777 West Bluemound Road
  P.O. Box 13819
  Milwaukee, WI 53213
  Phone: (414) 774-3630
  Fax: (414) 774-3259
  Email: halinfo@halleonard.com
  Internet: www.halleonard.com

CONTENTS

PREFACE

It was in Athens, at the start of a long Living Theatre tour, that I first came across Brecht's *Modellbuch* for ANTIGONE—an edition printed on postwar paper that was already crumbling in 1961, and has since gone to dust. It was a time of growing hopefulness that led to the enormous energy of 1968, a time of rising belief in the possibility of creating the world in which we all want to live, a time of optimism and vigorous resistance to the authoritarian aspects of the social structure which the violent past has left us as its legacy.

It was just after the apex of this violence, at the end of the Second World War, that Brecht created his first version of ANTIGONE in exile in Switzerland. In 1948, the first performances of the play were given in the Swiss city of Chur. Though it is said he was particularly interested in the figure of Antigone because he believed the role would serve as a useful preparation for Helene Weigel, in anticipation of her playing Mother Courage, Brecht was no doubt first drawn to ANTIGONE by the power of the ancient archetype: a woman alone defying the power of the state—a pungent parable for any time.

Through Sophocles, Brecht drew on the glory of the entire Hellenic enlightenment, whose thought, structure and poetry remain the play's foundation. But he also worked from the 1804 German translation of Sophocles' play by the quintessentially Romantic poet, Friedrich Hölderlin, from whom Brecht drew the sweep of his ANTIGONE's inflamed, lofty language, which demands of us the courage to exhort ourselves to our highest aspirations. And then Brecht himself developed the text in a direction that underscores the play's relevance to the Nazi debacle.

First of all, Brecht added a modern-day prologue in which two sisters (Antigone and Ismene) step out of a bomb shelter and, observing the ruin of the city, discuss the fate of their brother, a victim of the dictator's military machine. Within the text of the play proper, however, there are further Brechtian revisions. That Kreon's tyrannical refusal to act in accordance with humanitarian principles leads to the destruction of Thebes itself is largely a portent in the classical version. Brecht added an emphasis on the inevitable calamity spawned by political rigidity for which the fate of the Hitler regime clearly served as model. This is most evident in Brecht's use of the character of Kreon's son, Megareus, who is both commander of the armies gone after conquest as well as elder brother of the rebellious Hamon, captain of the home guard and betrothed to Antigone. Megareus is absent in the Sophoclean version, but Brecht (who appears to have drawn upon Euripides' THE PHOENECIANS for this version) brings him onstage for a blood-curdling monologue in which the dying soldier describes in chilling detail the fiery rout of the forces of the homeland. Thus Brecht attempts to anchor his play—which he himself titled THE ANTIGONE OF SOPHOCLES—as firmly in the history of this century as in the tales of the ancient world.

We knew at once that The Living Theatre ought to perform this play, because we are always searching for a next step that can take us along the trajectory of our commitment— to make blazingly clear in the best poetry the meaning of the Beautiful Nonviolent Anarchist Revolution—and Antigone is herself a clarion call to just such a Utopian vision. Interestingly, Brecht, ambivalent about the pacifist implications of the role of Antigone, writes in his preface to the *Modellbuch* that he regrets that she cannot truly represent the spirit of the German partisans who fought against the Nazis.

I translated ANTIGONE in Passaic County Jail during the 30 days that I spent there for refusing to surrender The Living Theatre on 14th Street to the assault police sent in by the government on the basis of charges that we owed the I.R.S. money—charges later proved false in a trial which Julian Beck and I conducted as a theatrical event.

In jail I had available all the books I needed: Brecht, Sophocles in Greek and in several English translations, Hölderlin, German, Greek and English dictionaries, other reference works—all stacked below the metal shelf the prison called my bed—as well as the cooperation of my 6 cell-mates, who agreed to allow my writing pads and manuscripts to occupy half of our common steel table, and who became my translation's first audience.

Afterwards I worked on the text for several years before we went into rehearsals in 1966 on the stage of the Berlin Akademie der Künste, searching for a style and much influenced by our work on Artaud. Jenny Hecht and I stood on a triangular stage and invented the first movements of Ismene and Antigone, the vision of the sublime French madman a-buzz in our bodies. The confrontation of the cerebral formulations of Brecht and Sophocles with the visceral passions of Artaud made ANTIGONE a powerful articulation of the meaning of those times. The Living Theatre performed ANTIGONE over a period of 20 years in 16 countries—and wherever we played it, it seemed to become the symbol of the struggle of that time and place—in bleeding Ireland, in Franco's Spain, in Poland a month before martial law was declared, clandestinely in Prague—the play is uncannily appropriate to every struggle for freedom, for the personal liberty that Antigone demands for herself.

There are myriad forms in which this text can be consummated. The Living Theatre's bare stage-Artaudian form is only one of many. As it yields to the sense of the contemporary politic, so ANTIGONE allows for an endless variety of production forms—the realistic, the surrealistic, the classical, the not-yet-dreamed-of—Antigone speaks with an ancient voice that is present wherever there is a willingness to speak out against conventional strictures and punitive laws, and to invoke the boundless human potential.

I would like to take this occasion to thank the many people who enabled The Living Theatre to bring Brecht's ANTIGONE to life for the first time in English, including Julian Beck, James Spicer, Pierre Biner, Stefan Brecht, Barbara Brecht-Schall, Ekkehard Schall, the editors at Suhrkamp Verlag, Glenn Young, the dozens of Living Theatre actors who have performed the play with me, and especially my husband, colleague and comrade, Hanon Reznikov.

Judith Malina
New York, January 1990

THE ANTIGONE LEGEND

by Bertolt Brecht
translated by Judith Malina

[*Brecht's poem, "The Antigone Legend," is a recapitulation of the drama in summary form. Brecht himself used it as a rehearsal device intended to develop objectivity in the actors' performances: his stage manager interrupted the rehearsal at intervals to read the relevant description of the action from the poem while the cast paused. The Living Theatre, on the other hand, used Brecht's poem for another purpose. Performing the play in English in different parts of the world, the company paused regularly to recite the poem's description of the action in the audience's own language.*

J.M.]

But Antigone, the child of Oedipus, went with the jug
to gather dust to cover the body of Polyneikes
which the angry tyrant had thrown to the dogs and the
    vultures.

And her sister Ismene met her as she was gathering dust.

Bitterly, Antigone complained of their brothers' fate,
both fallen in the war, the one a hero, the other,
fleeing the battle, slain, not by the enemy, but killed by his
    own men.

But she did not persuade her sister to take the forbidden
    steps
towards the shamed and mangled corpse of their brother.

And the sisters parted in anger at the break of day.

But hearing at dawn of the victory-battle in the long war for
    metal,
the Elders of Thebes put on the wreaths of victory,

which are woven of the glittering leaves of the poisonous
    laurel,
which confuses the senses and makes the step uncertain.

Early in the morning they were already standing in front of
    Kreon's house.

And back from the battle, preceding the troops of Argos,
came the tyrant, and found them in front of the house at
    daybreak.

And, leaning on the saber, he described how over in Argos
vultures now hopped from corpse to corpse; it delighted the
    elders.

Quickly they crowned him with laurel, but he did not yet
    give them
the saber, but grimly gave it to his bodyguard.

Reviling the son of Oedipus, his showpiece, to frighten the
    people,
the tyrant spoke of a bloody clean-up, exterminating the
    enemies
under the Theban roof, when a messenger came: the horror
had not horrified, the mangled body was covered with dust.

Angrily the tyrant questioned the guard and all the others,
and so that they saw it, he tested the saber's blade with his
    thumb.

Wandering with bowed heads, the Elders considered man
and his monstrous power, how the sea with the keel, and the
    beast
with the yoke, and the horse with the bridle were conquered,
and yet he will, like a monster, also conquer his fellow man.

And how, as Antigone was brought in and questioned as to
    why
she broke the law, she looked around and turned to the
    Elders
and saw that they were appalled and said: 'To set an
    example.'

Then she asked support from the Elders, but the Elders
looked to Kreon. Antigone said: 'He who seeks power
is drinking salt water. He can't keep it down, yet
he has to drink more. I am not the first sacrifice, nor the
    last.'
But they turned their backs. Antigone called: 'Woe is you!'

'She wants to divide us!' cried the tyrant, 'and divided,
our city will fall to the invaders.' Said Antigone: 'Always,
the men in power make this threat, and we bring you
    sacrifices, and soon
the city, thus weakened and enslaved, falls to the invader.
He who bows down sees only the earth and the earth will
    get him.'

'Fresh girl, are you cursing your country? Listen, it's thrown
    you out!'
Said Antigone: 'Who throws me out? A place where I can't
    hold my
head up isn't my country. O, there are less in the city
since you are in power. The youngsters, the men,
aren't they coming back? You left with so many and now you
    return
all alone.' Then the tyrant was silent and had no answer.

'You're raving,' said the Elders and asked, 'Haven't you
    heard of the victory battle?'
'Because she is my enemy,' said the tyrant, 'she begrudges
    you the victory.'
Said Antigone: 'It would be better, and safer too, to sit
in the ruins of our own houses, than with you in the enemy's
    city.'
The Elders looked at her coldly and stood by the tyrant.

And Ismene, her sister, came out of the house and said:
'I am the one who did it.' But Antigone said: 'She's lying.'
And wiping the sweat off, he said: 'Work it out between you.'

But Antigone was overcome by weakness, and asked her sister
to go on living. 'I think it is enough if I die.'

Said the tyrant: 'When joyous Thebes begins the dances

of peaceable Bacchus, the cave shall receive her, living and
  dead.

And they led her away, who dared to face up to the ruler.

Obediently, the Elders handed the ruler the mask of
  Bacchus,
speaking the choral song: 'When you dress up for the victory
  dances,
don't stamp too hard on the ground, and not where it grows
  green.'

'May he who has troubled you, praise your victory.'

And the ruler's youngest son stepped forward, Hamon,
commander of the city's garrison, who was to marry Antigone,
to bring news of the unrest in the city because of the fate of
  Oedipus' child.

Reluctantly now the father reveals his hidden distress
with a show of force and hardness, but his son does not
  understand him.

Not minding the listening Elders, and wooingly circling the
  stubborn one,
the father asks his son to forget her who broke the law.

But when his son did not yield, Kreon mocked him,
whipping the straw mane of his mask in his son's face.

And his son left him. The Elders watched with alarm.

Grimly the victor went to the celebration.

And the music from the city alarmed the listening Elders.
The dancers of Bacchus are forming their circles.

And this is the hour too when Oedipus' child in her room
hears Bacchus in the distance and prepares for her last
  journey.
For now he calls to his own, and the city, thirsting for
  pleasure,
gives the peaceable god its joyous answer.

For victory is great and Bacchus irresistible,
when he approaches the mourners and hands them the drink
    of forgetfulness.
Then she discards the black robes she was sewing tò mourn
    her sons in,
and runs to the orgy of Bacchus, seeking depletion.

And now, as Antigone was led out of Kreon's house,
she weakened at last and collapsed among her friendly
    servants.

Politely the Elders reminded her that she herself
chose her deeds and her death. She said: 'Are you making
    fun of me?'

And went on and complained of her fate: dreary childhood,
doomed parents, to whom she returns now, unmarried,
and also a brother who now draws her down to the grave.

The Elders set the bowl before her and the small jug of wine
    and
millet, the gifts for the dead, and recounted for her comfort
    the names
of the saints and heroes who died full of greatness and glory.

They sternly advise her to practice patience with godly
    resolution.

Then she got angry and called the Elders cowards.

And her own weakness vanished when she saw their
    weakness.
'You are expecting wagons' she cried, 'loaded with booty, and
    wagons
will come, but to carry booty away. You, the living' she cried,
'it is you whom I accuse' and tears of anger choked her.

And she looked around and saw beautiful Thebes'
roofs and hills and groves, and soberly bowed down before
    them,
taking her leave. But again her compassion turned to anger.

'Out of you, my native land, monsters have risen, and so you must
come to dust and ashes. Girls,' she said, 'if anyone
asks for Antigone, tell him: 'We saw her escape to the grave.'

Turned around and went, with light, secure steps.

Blindly the Elders watched her going, and recited the choral song:
'But she, too, once ate of the savory bread
that was baked in the dark caves. Not until her own kind
suffered and died, did she raise her voice loudly in protest.'

But she who warned them could not have yet reached the grave
when a somber awareness was sensed in the celebrant city.

For now the seer comes, the blind man, driven by rumors
of conflict in the ruler's house. And mocking, a mummer
leaps about him, and shakes the straw mane of the mask,
and rattles it over his head and pursues him across the plaza.
Lifting the sole of his foot to the tempo of the Bacchanalian dances,
he points a scornful thumb to show the elders the seer's failing.

Impudently tapping the ground with his staff before the seer's groping foot, and
it is Kreon, drunk with victory. The Elders watch in silence.

'Old fool, you don't seem to like celebrations. Why aren't you
wearing the laurel? It's ours!' And anger sharpened his voice.

'Does a blinder man follow the blind man?' asked the seer.
'Remember, Kreon, strife and sacrilege displease the gods.
Ugly birds rise up before me that have fed on Oedipus' son.'

The ruler laughed. 'I know that your birds fly at your pleasure,

obedient to your mood, and that your mood can be swayed by
  silver.'

'Please don't offer me any. What use is silver in wartime?'
said the seer. Said the ruler: 'The war is over.'

'Is it over?' asked the seer. 'Down by the harbor
they're drying fish for the troops, as though they won't be
  back by autumn.'
'You are cruel. Why? What mischief have you started?'
The tyrant stood silently by and had no answer.

And the seer got up and went.
And murmuring gloomily
the tyrant prepared to leave. The Elders watched
  astonished.
Fear answered fear, and they dared to ask the question:
'Well now, Kreon, how goes the war?' And he said, 'No
  good.'

And they stepped up to him, with the mask of peace in his
  hand,
and they too held the masks of peace in their hands.
And they argued with him whether it was their war or his.
'But it was you who sent me to get the metal in Argos!'
'But it was you who told us the victory was ours.' 'I said: In
  the end.'

And again he started to leave, and again the Elders
angrily pressed the ruler: 'Call the troops back home!'
because they were worried about the troops, and even more
  about their possessions.
And he drove the staff with the mask of peace into the
  ground.

'Certainly I'll call the troops, and my eldest son, Megareus,
will lead them, and, iron in hand, they will come to meet
  your ingratitude.'

And as the threatening name Megareus still hung in the air,
a messenger came: 'Sir, bow your head, Megareus

is no more, and your troops are besieged, and the enemy
   approaches.'

Gasping, he pictures the battle: how the troops, exhausted by
   brotherly
strife on account of Oedipus' son, half-heartedly lifted their
   spears,
while the people of Argos fought ferociously for their homes.

'And they come here ferociously now,' cried the messenger,
   and I'm
glad that I'm done for!' Held his stomach, and with fear on
   his face,
fell to the ground in front of Kreon's mask of peace.

But then Kreon screamed, too, but it was the father who was
   screaming.
Said the Elders: 'The enemy is advancing on us in fury, and
   Thebes,
drunk with joy, is dancing! Call up the troops of the home
   front!'

Then the Elders tore the victory wreaths from their heads,
and broke the masks of Bacchus, and covered the dead man
with the wreaths and masks and cried out: 'Woe is us!'

And the ruler remembered his other son, the younger one,
Hamon, leader of the troops of the home front,
and he hurried to forgive him and to pardon Antigone for
   him.

But the Elders stood up and struck the metallic cymbal
to waken the city from the deadly drunkenness of victory.
The stifling metal alarm disrupts the dancers of Bacchus,
and the stamping of triumph turns into terrified flight.

And through the raging city came a gentle messenger,
Antigone's youngest maid, who had led her to the grave.
'Hamon is dead and gone, bleeding by his own hand.
When he saw Antigone in the cave and saw that she was
   hanged,

he pierced himself with his sword in spite of the pleas of
 his father.'

And the Elders shudder to receive their leader, led by
Antigone's maids. He holds a bloody shirt in his hands.
'Hamon is dead and gone. Dead and gone is Thebes.
Because she betrayed me, she has become a meal for the
 vultures!'

And he showed the Elders the bloody shirt of his son,
who in anger denied him the sword. And rotten and gruesome,
unteachable, he staggers, he who was the leader of many,
toward the falling city. But the Elders
still follow the leader. Even now, in downfall and
 annihilation.

PROLOGUE

Berlin. April 1945

(Daybreak.
Two sisters come out of an air-raid shelter,
returning home.)

THE FIRST
> And when we came out of the air-raid shelter
> we saw that our house had not been destroyed, but
>   looked brighter
> than before, lit by the fire across the street; and then
> my sister was the one who saw it first.

THE SECOND
> Sister, why is our door open?

THE FIRST
> The fire-storm pushed it open.

THE SECOND
> Sister, what are these marks on the ground?

THE FIRST
> Only the footprints of someone who tried to escape.

THE SECOND
> Sister, what is that pack in the corner?

THE FIRST
> Better to find something there than to find something
>   missing.

THE SECOND
> It's a loaf of bread, sister, and a whole ham!

THE FIRST
> Well, that's nothing to be afraid of.

THE SECOND
> But sister, who was here?

THE FIRST
> How should I know?
>> Someone who wants us to have a good meal.

THE SECOND
> But we should have known! We have so little faith!
> What luck! Our brother is back!

THE FIRST
> And we embraced each other and we were happy
> because our brother was in the war and he was all right.
> And we cut up the ham and ate the bread
> that he brought for our needs.

THE SECOND
> Take more for yourself. The food is so bad
> in the factory lunchroom.

THE FIRST
> No, you need it more.

THE SECOND
> Take a bigger slice for yourself.

THE FIRST
> No, no more for me.

THE SECOND
> But how could he come here?

THE FIRST
> With the troops.

THE SECOND
> Where could he be now?

THE FIRST
> Wherever the battle is.

THE SECOND
> Oh.

THE FIRST
> But we couldn't hear any sound of battle.

THE SECOND
     I shouldn't have asked.

THE FIRST
     I didn't want to worry you.
     And as we were sitting there silently, a sound struck
     our ears from the other side of the door that froze our
          blood.
(*A scream from outside.*)

THE SECOND
     Sister, someone is screaming. Let's go see.

THE FIRST
     Sit down, you. If you see you'll be seen.
     So we didn't go to the door, and didn't see
     the things that happened outside.
     But we didn't eat anymore, and didn't look
     at one another. We stood up and got ready
     to go to work, as we did every morning.
     And my sister did the dishes and I
     remembered and took our brother's pack to the closet
     where his old things are kept.
     And there it was, as though my heart had stopped.
     There on a hook hung his field-jacket.
     Sister, he is not in the battle.
     He has run away.
     He is not in the war anymore.

THE SECOND
     There are some that are still in it. But he is not.

THE FIRST
     He must have been condemned to death.

THE SECOND
     And so he cheated them.

THE FIRST
     And there was a little hole....

THE SECOND
     And that was what he crawled through.

THE FIRST
>The others are still in it, but he is not in it.

THE SECOND
>He is not in the war anymore.

THE FIRST
>And we laughed and we were happy.
>Our brother was out of the war and he was all right.
>And we were still standing there when a sound struck
>our ears that froze our blood.

(*A scream from outside.*)

THE SECOND
>Sister, who's screaming outside the door?

THE FIRST
>They are torturing people again for whatever their
>reason.

THE SECOND
>Sister, shouldn't we go and see?

THE FIRST
>Stay inside, you. If you see, you'll be seen.
>So we waited awhile and didn't see
>the things that happened outside.
>But we had to go to work and then
>it was I who saw what was outside the door.
>Sister, sister, don't go out.
>Our brother is in front of the house.
>But he is not out of the thing.
>He is hanging from the butcher's hook. Ahh.
>But my sister did come out of the house
>and she screamed.

THE SECOND
>Sister, they have hanged him;
>that's why he called out to us.
>Give me the knife. Here, give me the knife
>so that I can cut him down so he won't hang there.
>So that I can carry his body inside
>and bring him back to life.

THE FIRST
>Sister, leave the knife alone.
>You won't bring him back to life.
>When they see us standing around him
>they'll do to us what they have done to him.

THE SECOND
>Let me go. I didn't go before
>when they hanged him.

THE FIRST
>Just as she reached the door
>the officer approached.
>>(*An officer enters.*)

OFFICER
>I know him, but who are you?
>He stepped out of your door.
>So I figure it can be proved
>that you and this traitor knew one another.

THE FIRST
>Please sir, don't arrest us.
>We don't know this person at all.

OFFICER
>Then what is she doing with the knife?

THE FIRST
>Then I looked at my sister.
>Would she now under the penalty of death
>try to free her brother?
>If only he had not died.

ANTIGONE

Outside Kreon's Palace.
Daybreak.

ANTIGONE (*gathering dust into an iron jar*)
    My sister Ismene, my twin,
        do you know of some form of madness,
    some labyrinth, some shame, or some useless labor
    that God has spared the twin
    orphans of Oedipus?
    In the long war, our brother Eteokles died for us: one
    among many who died young in the tyrant's service.
        But our brother
    Polyneikes was even younger when he saw his brother
        trampled
    to death under the hooves of the war-horse. In tears
    he fled from the unfinished battle; for others   10
    another decision is made by the spirit of battle, when
        with a hard
    blow with his right he unnerves his hand. Now
    the fugitive lurches forward
    until he has crossed the Dirsean river—breathing a
        sigh of relief
    at the sight of Thebes, his seven-gated city—when he
        is suddenly seized
    by blood-spattered Kreon, who killed his brother—
        standing behind them,
    lashing them all into his battle—and he is
        slaughtered.
    Have they told you or haven't they told you
    of the latest insults to be heaped
    on Oedipus' dwindling children?   20

ISMENE
    I haven't been to the market, Antigone.
    I've heard no news of our loved ones,
    neither loving words nor sad words;

and I'm not happier and I'm not sadder.

ANTIGONE

Then hear the news from me: and if your heart
stands still or pounds too hard,
because it's broken, then tell me so.

ISMENE

Gather your grey dust. It seems
you'd paint me blood-red words.

ANTIGONE

Here it is: our two brothers,   30
both dragged into Kreon's war for the grey iron ore
of distant Argos, and both killed,
are not both to be buried in the earth.
Of course the fearless hero of the battlefields,
        Eteokles,
shall, it is understood, be honored and buried
        according to custom;
but the other, Polyneikes, who died in disgrace
it is now said of his body
and it has been made known in the city, that no one
shall make a grave for him or mourn him.
He is to be left unmourned and unburied,   40
as a sweet meal for the vultures. And he
who does something about it is to be stoned to death.
Well, tell me; what are you going to do about it?

ISMENE

What are you doing, sister; testing me?

ANTIGONE

To see if you'll help me.

ISMENE

In what danger?

ANTIGONE

To bury him.

ISMENE

He, who has been denounced by the city?

ANTIGONE
>He, whom the city has renounced.

ISMENE
>He, who caused the revolt?   50

ANTIGONE
>Yes; my brother and yours.

ISMENE
>Sister, they'll catch you defenseless.

ANTIGONE
>But they won't catch me
>faithless.

ISMENE
>Poor thing. What drives you
>to drive the last of Oedipus' children
>all down to destruction?
>Forget the past.

ANTIGONE
>Because you are younger you've seen
>less horror. When we forget the past   60
>the past returns.

ISMENE
>And think of it this way: we're women,
>who haven't the strength to fight
>against men; and therefore we're obedient
>in this, and in some things even harder. Therefore
>I ask the dead and the oppressed to forgive me.
>When force is used against me, I obey
>the authorities. What's the sense of committing
>useless actions?

ANTIGONE
>I won't ask you again.   70
>Follow someone who gives orders. And do
>what you are ordered. But I
>am following the custom and burying my brother.
>And if I die for it? So what? I'll rest in peace
>among the peaceful. And I'll have left

something holy behind me. I prefer
to make friends in the underworld,
for I will live there forever. As for you,
laugh at shame and live.

ISMENE

Antigone, bitterly   80
hard as it is to live in disgrace, still
even the salt tears stop. They don't
flow from the eyes forever. The executioner's ax
puts an end to life's sweetness, but for the survivor
it opens the slow veins of pain. He can't stop
screaming; yet even while screaming, he hears
the birds swooping above him
and sees through curtains of tears the familiar
elms and rooftops of home.

ANTIGONE

I hate you. How shamelessly you show me   90
the tattered apron of your sentimentality. Right now
on the naked stones the flesh of your flesh is laid out
under the wide sky for the vultures. But you think
that was yesterday.

ISMENE

No, I'm not
good enough just to offer myself as a sacrifice, nor wilful
      enough.
And I'm afraid for you.

ANTIGONE

Don't give me advice! Live your life.
but let me at least do what I can to honor   100
those of us who have been shamed. I hope
that I'm not so particular that I couldn't bear
to die an unbeautiful death.

ISMENE

Go on and gather your dust. What you say is wrong,
but it's said in love, and beloved.

> (ANTIGONE *exits with the jar.* ISMENE *back into the*
> *house.* THE ELDERS *step forward.*)

THE ELDERS

> The wagons of booty are coming!
> The victory loaded with plunder
> to make Thebes forget the war!
> In the temples of all the gods,   110
> come out! And sing all night
> the choral songs. For Thebes is crowned with laurel
> and the Feast of Bacchus reigns...
> Here he comes from the battlefield,
> Kreon, Menokeus' son, who won us the victory.
> He brings news of the booty and promises us
> at last the return of the soldiers, for which he has
> > ordered
> and called together a council of The Elders of Thebes.
> > (KREON *comes out of the house.*)

KREON

> Gentlemen, tell the world: Argos
> is finished. The accounting was   120
> total. Only a few escaped
> from the eleven cities. Only the fewest.
> It is said of Thebes that when she's lucky
> she'll be luckier. But misfortune
> has not weakened you; rather you have weakened
> > misfortune.
> The thirst of our bloodthirsty weapons
> was quenched by the first taste of blood, but we did
> > not
> deny them repeated refreshment. On a rough resting
> > place,
> Thebes, you have laid down the men of Argos.
> > Without a city,
> Without a grave, out in the open, lies that which
> > defied you.   130
>
> Look over there
> where their city once stood!
> There you'll see dogs
> with shining faces.
> The great vultures circled her, screaming

from corpse to corpse,
but the meal was so rich
that the overfed birds couldn't rise from the ground.

THE ELDERS

You paint a pretty picture of great power,
and the city will love it when you deliver it;   140
and you cleverly add one more thing: the wagons
of plunder that drive through the streets full of
    booty.

KREON

Soon, friends, soon! But first to business! You haven't
yet seen me hang the ceremonial sword in the temple.
You see, I have called you together
for two reasons: first, because I know
that you will not count the costs
when it comes to oiling the wheels
of the man-mangling war-machine, any more
than you deny him the blood
of your sons in battle. However,
when they return, exhausted, to the comforts of
    home,   150
there is too much counting in the markets. Therefore
give me your quick assurance that the casualty-lists of
    Thebes
do not exceed the customary expectations. And also,
because the people of Thebes are always too quick to
    forgive,
now that the danger is over, they come here
to wipe the sweat off the homecoming hero
without asking whether that sweat is the sweat of
    the fever
of battle or only the cold sweat of fear, mixed with
the dust of desertion. Therefore, I have buried,
and I ask you to approve it, Eteokles,   160
who died for The State, with honors and laurels.
But the corpse of Polyneikes, his brother,
my nephew, and friend of the people of Argos,
shall lie unburied, as bare as this lies here.
He was the enemy: my enemy and Thebes'.

And therefore I want no mourning;
I want him to be left unburied,
to be devoured, as a meal, by dogs and vultures.
I have no respect for the man   170
who values human life more than his country.
But he who serves my State, dead or
alive, I'll praise him either way.
I hope you approve this.

THE ELDERS
    We approve it.

KREON
    And will you be responsible for carrying out the orders?

THE ELDERS
    A job like that is for the younger men.

KREON
    Not this job. The watch for the dead has started
        already.

THE ELDERS
    And are we to keep watch for the living?

KREON
    Yes, because there are some who are dissatisfied.

THE ELDERS
    There's no one here that's fool enough to risk his life.

KREON
    Not openly. But many have shaken their heads
    till they lost them
    —which brings me to this: we must do more.
    The State must be cleansed...
        (*Enter a* GUARD.)

THE GUARD
    Sir!
    I got here as fast as I could, out of breath to bring
    the message swiftly to our leader. Don't ask me why
    I couldn't make it any faster. My feet
    got ahead of my head, or else

my head raced on and dragged my feet behind; yet   190
no matter how tired I got, or how long I was
in the sun, out of breath, still
I kept going.

KREON

What is this breathlessness? Or
are you hesitating?

THE GUARD

I'm not holding anything back, so I ask myself why
        not
say it right out, since I didn't do it?
And I don't know anything. I don't even know
who did it to you. For me to draw conclusions
when I know so little   200
wouldn't mean a thing.

KREON

You look out for yourself. Your innocence,
my ambitious messenger, won't win you medals
for swift footwork.

THE GUARD

Sir,
you entrust your guards with great power. But
great power takes great effort.

KREON

Tell me your news and get out of here.

THE GUARD

I'll tell you my news. Just now, someone
buried the body. Sprinkled dust over the body   210
so that the vultures can't see him.

KREON

What? Who would dare undertake it?

THE GUARD

I don't know. There was no mark of a spade,
no sign of the use of a shovel. And the smooth ground
showed no wheel-marks. No sign of
the culprit. Wasn't a real grave,

just some soft dust, as though breaking the law
didn't take much.
But there were no animal tracks.
Not even a dog had come to tear and devour.   220
What the first light of day showed us
    struck us as unholy. And the lot
fell to me to bring our leader the message,
and nobody loves the bearer of bad news.

THE ELDERS

O Kreon, son of Menokeus, can it be
that something holy has happened here?

KREON

Stop that! Don't make me angrier yet by saying
that spirits pamper the cowards
who would cooly allow the pillars of their city's
    temples
and their sacrifices to be desecrated. There are some   230
in the city who hold certain things against me,
and complain that they will not bow
to my will. I know all about it;
they do it with bribes and presents.
Of all things graven,
there is nothing as evil as silver. It corrupts
whole states. It lures men from their homes
to practice every kind of godless action.
But I tell you, if you don't deliver
the person who did this, and in human form, alive,   240
bound to a board, and delivered, you will be hanged
and enter hell with a rope round your neck.
Then you'll learn how rewards are won.
Stop plundering each other and realize
that not all things are made for profit.

THE GUARD

Sir, a man in my position has a lot to be afraid of.
There are too many roads that lead to him,
being just a nobody whom you threaten. I'm less
afraid at the moment (well, always a little afraid)
of being accused of accepting bribes (though   250

if you suspect me, I'll turn my purse inside out
twice, to prove I have nothing)
than I fear to enrage you by contradicting you.
What I'm really afraid of is that this investigation
will get me a reward of rope round my neck; the
    hands of the powerful
more often provide my kind with rope than with
silver, as you well know.

KREON

Are you asking me riddles, you transparent fool?

THE GUARD

The dead man was of high rank and must have high-
    ranking friends.

KREON

Then go for their ankles if you   260
can't reach any higher! I know that there are
    troublemakers
everywhere. There are several who shudder to hear
of my victory and place the laurel wreath with
fear and trembling. I'll find them out.

THE GUARD

It's an unhealthy spot, where the mighty
have gotten into the hair of the mighty! I think
I'm still here. I wonder why.
    (Off)

THE ELDERS

There is much that is monstrous. But nothing
more monstrous than man.   270
Only he goes out on the sea at night
in winged whistling houses
when the south wind blows
against the winter.
And his ambitious plows tear up
the divine, holy earth,
the unspoilable and untiring;
year after year he drives his horses over the land.
He catches and hunts

the gently fashioned birds   280
and the wild beasts
and the salt-nourished life of the seas
with craftily slung nets,
the skillful man.
With cunning he catches the wild things
that forage at night in the hills.
He yokes the rough-maned stallion
and the untamed steer
that roams through the hills.
And he has mastered speech and the airy   290
flight of thought and the laws that order the State.
He has learned how to avoid
the polluted swamp air and
how to come in out of the rain. He knows it all
and yet is all unknown. He comes to nothing.
He always has advice.
Nothing is inadvisable for him.
Though all things are without boundaries for him
a limit has been set on him.
For he who finds no enemy becomes   300
his own enemy. As though he were an ox,
he yokes the neck of his neighbor, but his neighbor
tears it off. If he advances
he steps across the bodies of his own people. He can't
fill his own stomach. But he builds a wall
around his property; and the wall:
It must be torn down! Open the roof to the
rain! He counts what is human
as nothing at all. He has become
his own monster.   310

     O, I am tempted by heaven
not to admit that I know her.
It isn't she. Antigone,
unfortunate child of an unfortunate
father, Oedipus' child, what brings you
to this place as a criminal
under the laws of The State?
(*Enter* THE GUARD, leading ANTIGONE)

THE GUARD
>Here she is; she did it. We caught her
>as she made the grave. Where's Kreon?

THE ELDERS
>He's coming out.   320
>>(KREON *comes out of the house*)

KREON
>What are you bringing her here for? Where did you
>>catch her?

THE GUARD
>She made the grave. Now you know everything.

KREON
>Who is she? That you cover her face?   322a

THE GUARD
>Because of the shame. Because she did it.   322b

KREON
>I hear your words. But did you yourself see it?

THE GUARD
>Just as she started the grave, against your orders.
>When you're lucky you can speak clearly.

KREON
>Give me the story.

THE GUARD
>It was like this: After I left you,
>as you made those terrible threats,
>we wiped the dust off the body,
>which was putrifying already; and we sat   330
>on a hill where there was air, because the smell
>of the dead man was strong. And we agreed
>that if we got sleepy we'd wake each other with a
>>poke
>of the elbows. We opened our eyes
>because a sudden warm wind
>lifted the mist from the ground
>and whirled it along the fringe of the forest,

tearing the hair of the woods into the valley,
filling the air with fog, so that we had to blink,
yes, that was it, and rub our eyes; it was then   340
that we saw her, standing there crying out
In a sharp voice like a bird that mourns
when it sees the empty nest, without young ones.
She wailed because she saw the dead man naked;
and she spread the dust over him again,
out of the iron jug. Three times she sprinkled
dust on the dead man. We ran and held her,
and she didn't resist. And we accuse her
of these present things that we have witnessed.
But she denied nothing and was   350
gentle toward me and sad at the same time.

KREON

Do you admit or do you deny that you did it?

ANTIGONE

I say that I did it and I don't deny it.

KREON

Now tell me, and be brief:
are you aware of what was announced
in the open city about this particular corpse?

ANTIGONE

I knew it. How could I help it. It was clear enough.

KREON

And yet you dared to break my law?

ANTIGONE

Just because it was your law, a human law,
that's why a human being may break it—and   360
I am just as human as you and only slightly more
        mortal. And if
I die before my time, I think it's
because it has its advantages; when you've lived
the way I have, surrounded by evil, isn't there some
slight advantage in death? And further, if I had let
        my mother's
dead son lie unburied,

that would have made me unhappy; but this
does not make my unhappy. And if I seem crazy to you
because I fear the judgement of heaven,
which hates the bared sight of mangled bodies,   370
and I don't fear your judgement,
then let a crazy judge judge me.

THE ELDERS
Tough child of a tough father:
she hasn't learned how to be cautious.

KREON
The toughest iron yields
and loses its stubbornness, tempered
in the ovens. It happens every day.
But this one here enjoys
making fun of the laws of the land.
And to top this impertinence, now that   380
she's done it, she laughs about it and boasts
that she's done it. I hate that: when somebody's
caught in a crime and tries to make it look pretty.
And yet, though she insults me in spite of our family
     ties,
I'll be slow to condemn her because of our family ties.
Therefore I ask you: since you did it in secret
and now it's out in the open, wouldn't you say,
to avoid severe punishment, that you're sorry you did
     it?
     (ANTIGONE *is silent*)

KREON
Tell me why you're so stubborn.

ANTIGONE
To set an example.   390

KREON
Doesn't it matter to you that I have you in my hands?

ANTIGONE
What more can you do to me, since you have me, than
     kill me?

KREON
>   Nothing more. But having this, I have all.

ANTIGONE
>   What are you waiting for? I don't like
>   what you're saying and I won't like what you're going
>   to say.
>   And I know you don't like me either.
>   Thought there are those who do, because of what I
>   did.

KREON
>   So you think there are others who see things as you
>   do?

ANTIGONE
>   They see it too and they are moved by it.

KREON
>   Aren't you ashamed to claim their support without
>   asking?   400

ANTIGONE
>   There's nothing wrong in honoring my brother.

KREON
>   But the one who died for his country was also your
>   brother.

ANTIGONE
>   Yes. Both were my brothers. We are all of one family.

KREON
>   And the coward? Do you love him as much as the
>   other?

KREON
>   He who was not your slave is dearer to me than a
>   brother.

KREON
>   Of course, if good and evil are the same as one
>   another.

ANTIGONE

    The things are not the same: to die for you or to die
        for one's country.

KREON

    Wasn't there a war?

ANTIGONE

    Yes. Your war.

KREON

    Not the country's?   410

ANTIGONE

    A strange country. It wasn't enough for you
    to rule over the brothers in their own city.
    How beautiful Thebes was when we lived
    under the trees, in peace and unafraid. But you
    had to drag them all the way to Argos, so you could
        rule
    over them there too. And you turned one of them into
        the
    butcher of peaceful Argos. But the scared one
    you lay out to feed the vultures and frighten his
        loved ones.

KREON

    I advise you to say nothing. Don't say anything
    to defend her. If you know what's good for you.   420

ANTIGONE

    But I will appeal to you, for if you help me in my
        trouble
    it will help you later. The man who's after power is
        like
    the thirsty man who drinks salt-water; he can't hold
        it in,
    but he has to have more. Yesterday it was my
        brother. Today it is I.

KREON

    I am waiting
    to see who stands by you.

ANTIGONE (*Since the Elders are silent*)
>   And you take it and let him shut you up.
>   It will be remembered.

KREON
>   She's keeping accounts!
>   Dissension. That's what she wants under the Theban
>   roof.   430

ANTIGONE
>   You who cry for unity live by conflict.

KREON
>   I live by conflict here and on the Argive battlefield.

ANTIGONE
>   That's right. That's how it is. Anyone who uses
>   violence
>   against his enemy will turn and use violence against
>   his own people.

KREON
>   It seems the dear girl wouldn't grudge me to the
>   vultures.
>   And what if Thebes fell, through our conflict,
>   to be devoured by the invaders?

ANTIGONE
>   The men in power always threaten us with the fall
>   of The State.
>   It will fall by dissension, devoured by the invaders;
>   and so we give in to you, and give you our power, and
>   bow down;   440
>   and, because of this weakness, the city falls and is
>   devoured by the invaders.

KREON
>   Are you accusing *me* of throwing the city away to be
>   devoured by the enemy?

ANTIGONE
>   The city threw herself away by bowing down before
>   you.

because when a man bows down he can't see what's
 coming at him.
He only sees the earth—and ooh! she will get him.

KREON

Insult the whole earth, you monster, insult your
 country!

ANTIGONE

Wrong. Earth is an ordeal. But my country is not only
 the earth, or the house built by sweat that
 stands
helplessly in the path of the fire, not a place
where I can't hold my head up. I claim that's not my
 country.   450

KREON

Does it claim and not protect you?   450a
Your country no longer claims you as her own,
but throws you out like the polluting filth that dirties
 all it touches.

ANTIGONE

Who throws me out? There are less in the city
since you rule it. And there will be still less.
Why do you come alone? You left with many.

KREON

Who's missing?

ANTIGONE

Where are the youngsters? The men? Aren't they
 coming back?

KREON

How she lies! Everyone knows they stayed behind
only to clear the battlefields of the last weapons.

ANTIGONE

And to do your last mischief   460
and become a horror, till their own fathers
wouldn't recognize them when
they are finally killed like beasts of prey.

KREON

    She's insulting the dead!

ANTIGONE

    How stupid you are! I'm in no mood
    for winning arguments.

KREON

    When have I ever concealed the sacrifice made for
        the victory?   467a

THE ELDERS

    Pity her. Don't hold her words against her.
    But you in your ravings, don't let your tragedy make
        you
    disparage Thebes' glorious victory.

KREON

    But she doesn't want the people of Thebes to live in
        the houses of Argos. She'd rather   470
    see Thebes destroyed.

ANTIGONE

    We would sit more safely
    in the ruins of our own city, than with you
    in the enemies' houses.

KREON

    There, she said it! You heard it!
    She breaks every law, knows no limits, like a guest
    reluctant to leave, who insolently
    tampers with his luggage.

ANTIGONE

    I only took what is mine. And I had to steal that.   480

KREON

    You see as far as your nose. But you don't see
    The State's divine order.

ANTIGONE

    It may well be divine, but I'd rather
    that it were human, Kreon, son of Menokeus.

KREON

>Get out. You were always our enemy and even in hell
>>you shall be so;
>like the mangled one, you shall be hated even in
>>hell, you nothing.

ANTIGONE

>Who knows what the customs are down there?

KREON

>The enemy, even when dead, does not become a
>>friend.

ANTIGONE

>Of course he does. I don't live to hate, but to love.

KREON

>Then go to hell, if you want to love,   490
>and love down there. Under my rule,
>your kind don't live long.
>>(*Enter* ISMENE)

THE ELDERS

>But now Ismene comes,
>the sweet one, who is for peace.
>Her face is washed
>with tears and flushed with pain.

KREON

>Yes! You! You stay inside. Get home. I have
>brought up two monsters. A pair of snakes.
>Come, out with it.
>Did you take part at the grave, or are you innocent? 500

ISMENE

>I did it. If my sister will accept me.
>I took part too, and I accept my guilt.

ANTIGONE

>But your sister won't let you.
>She didn't want to. I didn't take her with me.

KREON

>Fight it out! I don't bicker over small things.

ISMENE

    I'm not ashamed of my sister's misfortune,
    and I'm asking her to call me her accomplice.

ANTIGONE

    By all who are beyond the world of matter
    and who talk together down in hell: 510
    I don't like those who love with words alone.

ISMENE

    Sister, not everyone is good enough for sacrifice,
    but even I am good enough for death.

ANTIGONE

    Don't die too abstractly. Don't meddle in things
    that are none of your business. My death is enough.

ISMENE

    My sister is too strict. I love you.
    If she is gone, what would I have to love?

ANTIGONE

    There's Kreon. Love him. Be his. I'm leaving you.

ISMENE

    Does it amuse my sister to make fun of me?

ANTIGONE

    Maybe it hurts too, and the cup of my pain runneth
        over.   520

ISMENE

    But what I said still goes.

ANTIGONE

    That would be nice. But I've made my decision.

ISMENE

    Is it because you did it without me, that you can die
        without me?

ANTIGONE

    Be of good cheer and live. I have a dead soul,
    sister, and I am only of use to the dead.

KREON

>These women, I tell you they're all alike;
>one of them loses her mind, and another one follows.

ISMENE

>I can't live without her.

KREON

>We're not talking about her. She doesn't exist.

ISMENE

>But you're killing your own son's bride.   530

KREON

>There's more than one field for a man to plow.
>Get ready to die. And so that you'll know exactly
>when it's going to happen: when drunken Thebes
>invites me to the dance of Bacchus. Get
>rid of these women.
>>(THE GUARD *exits into the house with* ANTIGONE
>>*and* ISMENE. KREON *orders his bodyguard to*
>>*deliver the sword*)

AN ELDER (*accepting the sword*)

>When you dress up for the victory dances, don't stamp
>on the ground too hard, and not there where it grows
>>green;
>may he who has troubled you, mighty one,
>praise you.

THE ELDERS

>>(*Giving* KREON *the sceptre of Bacchus*)
>Don't drive him down so deep   540
>that he's out of sight,
>for he lies in that direction, on the ground,
>naked to confront you. He is resigned
>to his shame, hideous and horrified,
>abandoned to his loss, dehumanized, he remembers
>his earlier form and rises and is new.

THE ELDERS

>Patiently the brothers of Lachmyia sat in their fire-
>>gutted house.

rotting away; they earned their bread by weaving,
    and the ice
froze over them each winter, and their women
didn't live there at night, but furtively sat around   550
all day in their scarlet cloaks. And always
the threatening cliff beckoned to them.
But not until Peleas came,
dividing them with his sceptre, parting them,
    touching them
ever so lightly, could they rise up...
and kill all their oppressors.
for that was the last straw for them; for often the
    sum of misery
must only be rounded out by a fraction; and then the
    blind
sleep, full of moaning with prehistoric exhaustion,
    comes to an end.   560
Slowly and swiftly, the moons wax and wane
unevenly, and all the while
evil is growing, and now
the last light
falls on the last root of Oedipus' house.
And when the great fall, they don't fall alone,
they fall on many, as when, below us on the Pontian
    sea,
the ill-blowing
winds of Thrace in the salty night
tear up a hut, and, lifted from the ground, it whirls
along the dark and dishevelled shore,   570
and the groans roar from the stricken coast.

      Hamon is coming, your youngest
      son, dismayed
      at the loss of Antigone.
      His young bride lies stricken
      on her dread bride bed.
      (*Enter* HAMON)

KREON
    Son, there's a rumor you've come
    to speak of that young woman, not to your ruler

but to your father; and if that's so   580
you've come for nothing. When we returned from the
    battle,
which went well, through blood and sacrifice,
she was the only one who did not welcome us,
    begrudging
our side the victory. She busies herself with only one
    matter,
and that one rotten.

HAMON

Nevertheless, I come to you
about this thing and hope that my father
will not listen with anger when his son's voice
is the one that must bring
bad news to the ruler.   590

KREON

When a man brings up fresh children
it can be said that his efforts bring him only
the laughter of his enemies. The bitter
pill cures. That's why it's prescribed.

HAMON

You govern many people, but if you'll listen
only to good news, don't
stay in command; let go
of the helm, if you don't want to steer, and drift!
The people are afraid of your name. Therefore
when big fires burn, you get small messages.   600
But there is this advantage to family ties:
we don't hold each other to account so strictly. And
    many
faults are readily forgiven, and so we often hear
the truth from members of our family
because we can restrain our anger towards them.
My brother, Megareus, can't come to tell you
because he fought at Argos and has not come back
and doesn't know what fear is, so I have to tell you.
Listen: there is deep dissatisfaction in the city.

KREON

> You listen: when my flesh and blood turns rotten   610
> it nourishes my enemy. The uncommitted man
> who doesn't know his mind tastes dissent
> in every small annoyance. One complains of taxes,
> another wants to end conscription;
> but I keep them both separated and in my power
> because I have the weapons. But when
> there are loopholes and the government seems
>   divided
> and wavers and is indecisive, then
> the stone can start rolling until
> it threatens the house that's already surrendered.
>   Speak   620
> but I'll listen only to him whom I brought up,
> my son, to whom I taught the strength of the spear.

HAMON

> There is some truth in everything. There is a saying:
> "Test the strength of thy tongue on the anvil of
>   truth." She
> who didn't want the merciless dogs
> to devour her brother: the city
> is with her in this. Although they condemn
> the dead man's crimes.

KREON

> It's not enough. I call that weakness.
> No, the filth that I've cut off is not enough.   630
> It must be done in public, so that other filth
> will not forget how I cut off the filthy.
> And that they see that my hand will not miss its
>   mark.
> But you, knowing little of the case,
> knowing nothing, you advise me: watch your step,
> look for alternatives, talk to them in their terms,
> as if authority could sway the many-bodied masses
> to difficult deeds by being
> nothing but a small, cowardly ear.

THE ELDERS
>But it saps the strength to think up cruel
>>punishments.   640

KREON
>To crush the curse to earth, until it curses, requires
>>strength.

THE ELDERS
>But the gentle uses of order can do much.

KREON
>There are many orders, but who gives the orders?

HAMON
>Even if I were not your son I'd say: you do.

KREON
>If I am charged with it, I'll do it my way.

HAMON
>Do it your way, but make it the right way.

KREON
>Not knowing what I know, you can't know what it is.
>Are you my friend no matter how I do it?

HAMON
>I want you to do it so that I can be your friend.
>But don't say you alone can be right, and no other.   650
>He who cuts himself off from the others has
>no thoughts or speech or soul like another,
>and if we look inside such a man
>we would find him empty; but another kind of man,
>if there is such a wise man somewhere, is not
>>ashamed
>to keep on learning and not carry anything to
>>extremes.
>>Look, when the rain-swollen brook gushes
>>past the trees, how all those that bend
>>are spared, but the unyielding
>>are broken. Or when a laden ship   660
>>spreads out her sails and won't slacken,

bending back from the rower's bench,
how it must end in shipwreck.

THE ELDERS

Give in—when the spirit demands it. Give us change.
And change us. And if we shudder in our humanity,
then shudder with us.

KREON

Shall we prepare ourselves
for the slavedriver's chains? Is that what you want?

HAMON

And the chained,
When a certain stench reaches their nostrils,   670
the drudgery driven may rise up and wonder
where they are being driven, and driven so hard,
and drag us all down into the abyss with all the
    wheels and chains.
Know that the city is torn by doubts.
What peace threatens, war deranges.

KREON

The war is over. Thanks for the instructions.

HAMON

Then too, I have heard the suspicion
that you have the intention of preparing
for the victory celebration with a bloody
housecleaning of all who have offended you.   680

KREON

By whom? Your reward was here. Much greater
than if you choose only to be a spokesman, babbling
so suspiciously about suspicion.

HAMON

Forget her.

THE ELDERS

Of the virtues of leadership
the most useful is called: forgive and forget.
Let go of the past.

KREON

> Since I'm part of the past
> I find forgetting difficult. But you,
> couldn't you, if I ask you,   690
> forget her whom you're defending,
> lest those who long for my downfall whisper,
> "He seems to be that woman's comrade."

HAMON

> Not only hers, but of all that's just, wherever I see it.

KREON

> Wherever there's a hole in it.

HAMON

> Insults won't stop
> my concern for you.

KREON

> Your bed is still empty.

HAMON

> I'd call that stupid if it wasn't my father that said
>   it.

KREON

> I'd call that fresh if it weren't a woman's slave who
>   said it.

HAMON

> Better her slave than yours.

KREON

> Now it's out and can't be retracted!

HAMON

> And it won't be. You want to say everything
> and hear nothing.

KREON

> That's how it is. And now get   704a
> out of my sight. Go like the coward who   704b
> spares himself too, in the hour of decision.   704c
> Take that brat away. Quickly.

HAMON
> And I'll get away. So that you need not look
> at a man who is not afraid and makes you tremble.
> (*He exits*)

THE ELDERS
> Sir, he who went out angry is your youngest son.

KREON
> But he won't rescue those women from death.

THE ELDERS
> Then you're thinking of killing them both?   710

KREON
> No, not the one who stayed away, you're right.

THE ELDERS
> And the other one, how will you kill her?

KREON
> Lead her out of the city, where now the dances
> of Bacchus are lifting the feet of my people. Put her
>   guilt
> away where there are no people to see her. Put her,
> alive, into the cave in the cliffs. With millet and
>   wine, the only
> meal that is fit for the dead, as though she were
>   buried.
> Those are my orders.
> So that in the end my city shall not bring me shame.
>   (KREON *exits to the city*)

THE ELDERS
> Now I seem to see it clouding my vision,   720
> that this is the hour when Oedipus' child in her
>   room
> hears Bacchus in the distance and prepares for her
>   last journey.
> Now he calls on his people, always thirsting for
>   pleasure;
> and our city woefully gives him the joyous answer;
> for victory is great and Bacchus irresistible.

When he approaches the mourners he hands them
      the drink of forgetfulness,
And the city discards the black robes she was sewing
      to mourn her sons
and runs to the orgy of Bacchus in search of
      depletion,
      (THE ELDERS *take their Bacchus staffs*)
O lusts of the flesh, it is you
who win every battle! Even incestuous   730
lovers are overwhelmed by your urging.
He never feels empty who gives himself over to be it,
not only to feel it. Possessed, he is at peace; and he
yields himself to the yoke and bares
his neck, not afraid of
the fumes of the salt-mines or the thin-
walled ship on the black waters. He mixes
alien skins and tosses
them all together, yet never despoils
the bounteous earth with violent hands, but   740
peacefully from the first act of creation is
      companioned
with concord and great conciliations. Because beauty,
      who never
is warlike, is holy and joins in the games.
      (ANTIGONE *enters, led by* THE GUARD *and followed
      by* MAIDS)

AN ELDER
      But now I find myself losing
      the rhythm, and I can't hold back
      the welling of tears, for now
      Antigone comes to receive
      the gifts of earth, the wine and the millet.

ANTIGONE
      Men of my city—look at me
      take my last steps   750
      and my last look
      at the sunlight.
      And never again?
      He beds us all alike, the god of death.

He is leading me alive
to the harbor of his river.
No wedding for me. For me
no wedding-song. I am
the Bridge of Acheron.

THE ELDERS

But your going is famous; praises go with you, as
          you   760
go into this death chamber.
No illness consumed you, nor were you
the victim of hard labor
for hard wages. You would not accept such wages.
Living your life, you go alive
down into death.

ANTIGONE

Oh no! They're making fun of me!
Yes, of me, and I'm not even dead yet,
and I still see the daylight.
My city! and oh, my city's   770
wealthy men! you must, yes, must
bear witness for me, of how and why I go unmourned
by those who love me, and under what
laws I must go
into an unheard of grave. I,
who do not belong to the shadows,
nor to man's mortality;
I, who belong to life, not to death.

THE ELDERS

When you're up against power
you can't expect pity.
Violence never examines its motives.

ANTIGONE

O my father, O my unhappy mother,
of whom I was born in anguish,
and to whom I return cursed
to lodge without a husband.
O, O my brother,
how sweet life is, and you've lost it.

Me too, I'm all that's left.
Draw me close down to you.

THE ELDERS (*Putting a bowl of millet down in front of her*)
 The body of Danae too, had to endure   790
 the iron gate, instead of the light
 of heaven. She lay in the dark prison,
 though she too came of a mighty race, child.
 She counted the strokes of the golden hours
 for the creator of time.

ANTIGONE
 I've heard how pitifully
 the Phrygian girl,
 Tantalos' daughter, died
 in the tower of Sipylos,
 bent beneath wreaths of ivy gathered slowly among
   the stones.   800
 And men say that winter is always with her
 and her throat is washed
 with the snowbright tears of her eyelids. It may be
 that I, like her, go to a sanctified bed.

THE ELDERS (*Putting a bowl of wine in front of her*)
 Her speech is holy, but then she is witness to
   holiness,
 while we are of this world and witness to
   worldliness.
 Yes. You perish, but greatness is yours,
 and not unlike holy sacrifice.   810

ANTIGONE
 And so you sigh and give me up for lost.
 How piously you gaze upwards at the blue heavens,
 but you don't look me straight in the eye.
 And yet, I've only done what's holy.

THE ELDERS
 They caught the son of Dryas loudly
 and rapturously protesting against the injustice of the
   tyrant
 Dionysus, and with stones

they stoned him to death and he got to know God
in his madness, with his shrieking voice.

ANTIGONE

And it would be better too, if you   820
gathered together and the protests against injustice
        and dried
them of tears and did something useful with them.
        You
don't look far enough.

THE ELDERS

But on the chalky cliffs with
the sea on both sides, at the mouth of the Bosphorus,
there, near the city, the war god watched as two
Phineans, who saw all too far,
had their eagle eyes pierced through
with spears, and it was dark
in their brave eyes' circles.   830
For the power of fate is frightful;
neither riches nor valor appease him,
nor towers escape him.

ANTIGONE

I beg you don't talk about fate;
I know all about that. Speak of him
who kills me, although I am innocent; he
has a shove coming from fate! Don't think
that you're safe. You're really the victims.
More mangled bodies
will be heaped up for you, unburied as a cairn   840
for the unburied. You, who dragged Kreon's war
across distant frontiers, though you may
win battles, the last one
will destroy you. You, who called for booty, you
will not see full wagons, but
empty ones. I mourn for you, survivors,
—what you will see
when my eyes will be filled with dust! Lovely
        Thebes,
my homeland, my city; and you, Dirsean River

that circles Thebes, where the   850
wagons draw up; oh, you woods!...my voice falters to
      say what
will become of you. You have spawned
the inhuman. Therefore
you must come to dust. Tell
any one who asks about Antigone that
you saw her escape to her death.
                (ANTIGONE *exits with* THE GUARD *and* THE MAIDS)

THE ELDERS
            Turned around and went, with broad steps, as
                  though
            she led her guards. Across the plaza there
            she went, where the victory columns
            had already been erected. Then she went faster,
            vanished.   860
But she too once
ate of the bread that was baked by slaves
in the dark cliffs. She sat still in the shade
of the prison towers that shelter sorrow, till all
that had left the deadly doors of Labdacus' house
re-entered dead. The bloody hand
deals out to each his own, and
they don't just take it, they grab it.
Only thereafter she lay   870
rebellious in her freedom,
thrust into the good.
The cold awakens her.
Not until the last
of her patience was exhausted and the last
crime measured would Oedipus' unseeing child
remove the customary blindfold from her eyes
to look at the abyss that surrounds her.
Just as blindly now
Thebes lifts its feet and giddily   880
tastes the victory libation of highly-spiced
herbs concocted in the darkness
and swallows it, and exults.

Here comes Tiresias, the blind man, the seer,
    driven
by rotten rumors of growing dissension
and the simmering unrest below.
(*Enter* TIRESIAS, *led by a child, and followed by*
KREON)

TIRESIAS

Always go gently, child, go steadily and be
untroubled by the dancers; you're
leading. Leaders
shouldn't follow Bacchus.   890
He who lifts his heels too high from the ground
can't avoid falling.
And look out for the
victory-columns. Victory!
they scream in the city,
and the city is full of fools!
See the blind
follow the seeing, but the blind
are followed by the blinder.

KREON (*who has followed him, mocking*)
Why are you mumbling
against the war, you treasonable fool.

TIRESIAS

Because you are dancing
before you have won it, unreasonable fool.

KREON

Stubborn and senile, you're a seer who sees only
what doesn't exist, but
you don't see the victory-
columns that tower around us.

TIRESIAS

Can't see 'em. And my reason's
not twisted. That's why I'm here,
dear friends. I don't even recognize the thick
laurel leaves, before
they are withered and rattle

or I bite into them and taste
the bitterness and I know that's the laurel.

KREON

You don't like celebrations. That's why you
speak to us with a terrible tongue.

TIRESIAS

I have seen terrible things. Listen to the bird-
oracles and what they portend for Thebes,
drunk with premature victory and deafened
by the droning shouts of the Bacchus dancers. I sat   920
on an ancient chair in a harbor full of birds.
And I heard a murderous turbulence rise in the air
    above me.
And there was the lashing fury of scratching claws
as the birds butchered each other. Frightened,
I quickly tested the newly-lit altars, but
not in a single spot could I make a good fire. Only
    smoke
waltzing tearfully skyward and the thighbones of
    the sacrificial ox
jutting out of the fat meant to cover it.

THE ELDERS

Very bad signs on the day of victory,
and news that kills joy.   930

TIRESIAS

This is the deadly meaning of the sinister symbols:
it is you, Kreon, who cause the city's sickness,
because the altars and hearths
are profaned by dogs and vultures who are satisfying
their hunger indecently on the body of Oedipus'
    fallen son.
Therefore the birds don't sing their song
of good omen, because they have eaten the flesh
of a dead man. But the gods don't care
for the taste of such smoke. Therefore soften
your heart towards the dead man and stop your
    persecution   940
of the dead.

KREON
>Your birds, old man,
>fly very nicely for you. I know about that. I wish
>>they would
>fly as nicely for me. I am not altogether so
>>unschooled
>in this business of the prophetic arts,
>thought I'm not so greedy. So pocket
>your treasures from Sardis and your Indian gold.
>But know this: I will not bury the corpse
>and I am not afraid of heaven's wrath.
>Man doesn't bother the gods, that much I know.   950
>But listen, old man, many mortals
>even among the very powerful
>come to a very grim end when
>they make up grim stories for the sake of profit.

TIRESIAS
>I am too old to compromise myself
>for the short time that's left to me.

KREON
>No one is so old
>that he doesn't want to grow older.

TIRESIAS
>I know.
>But I know more.   960

THE ELDERS
>Say it, Tiresias.
>Sir, let the seer be heard.

KREON
>Say it, by all means, but let's make a bargain.
>The prophet likes to profit from his prophecy in
>>silver.

TIRESIAS
>I heard that that's what tyrants have to offer.

KREON
>Even when they're blind,

they'll bite into the coin to tell
if it's silver.

TIRESIAS

I don't want you to offer me any
because in wartime no one knows what he'll keep,   970
whether it's silver, or sons, or power.

KREON

The war is over.

TIRESIAS

Is it?
I'll ask you a question.
Since, according to you, I know nothing,
I'll have to ask. Since you tell me I can't see
into the future, then I must see
into the present and into the past to stay
within my art and still be a seer. Of course, I
only see what a child sees: that the victory-columns 980
are stripped bare of metal. I say that's because
        they're still
making spears. That furs are being sewn
for the troops, I say: as if Autumn were coming.
And that fish are being preserved: as if for winter
        rations.

THE ELDERS

I thought that was before the victory battle,
and is now discontinued. Won't booty
come with metal and fish now from Argos?

TIRESIAS

And there are many guards, and whether they guard
much or little, no one knows. But there is much
confusion in your house and no amnesties granted   990
as is customary after happy occasions. And it is said
that your son Hamon left you in anger
because you have entombed Antigone, his bride, in a
        cave,
because she tried to open a grave
for her brother Polyneikes,

because you struck him down and left him unburied,
because he turned against you,
because your war killed his brother, Eteokles.
That's how you're cruelly bound up with cruelty.
And since I'm not silenced by silver I'll ask   1000
the second question: why are you so
cruel, Kreon, son of Menokeus? I'll make it easier:
is it because there's not enough metal for your war?
What is it that you've done, both mad and bad,
that now you must compound both madness and
          badness?
Half-tongued were worse
But I'll give my double answer. It is: none.
And I put none and none together and say,
mismanagement cries for greatness and finds: none.   1010
War escalates and breaks its leg.
Theft follows theft and need breeds need,
and more means more and in the end it's: none.
And so I have looked back, and I have looked
          around,
and I have looked ahead and shuddered.
Child, take me away from here.
          (TIRESIAS *exits, led by the child*)

THE ELDERS
          Sir, if my hair
          had still been black, it would now
          have turned white. That angry man
          has said terrible things,   1020
          and left still more terrible things unsaid.

KREON
          And I say: why
          bring us what's better left unsaid?

THE ELDERS
          Kreon, son of Menokeus, when
          are the young men returning to
          the city now empty of men, and how
          goes your war, Kreon, son of Menokeus?

KREON

> Since that troublemaker has directed your eyes
> to this matter, I'll tell you: the dirty war
> that Argos started is not   1030
> yet over and doesn't go
> too well. When I announced peace,
> there was only one little detail missing and that
> only because of Polyneikes' treason.
> But he has been punished
> and so has she who mourned him.

THE ELDERS

> And this too is not
> at an end: he has turned
> against you, he who leads
> the strength of your spears here at home, your
> youngest son, Hamon.   1040

KREON

> I no longer want him
> at all. Get him out of my sight
> and yours; he deserted me
> for trivial thoughts of his bed.
> My son Megareus still fights for me; my son
> sends endless thrusts against
> the weakened walls of Argos
> with the armoured youths of Thebes.

THE ELDERS

> They are not expendable,   1050
> Kreon, son of Menokeus,
> We have always followed you. And there was order
> in the city, and you kept the enemy from our throats.
> But now, under the Theban roofs, the thieves
> who have nothing and thrive on war,
> and those who live on discord, the rabble-rousers
> with empty stomachs and strong lungs in the market
>   place,
> talking because they are paid or because they are not
>   paid,
> now they are shouting again, and they have

some strong material too; have you   1060
started something too big, son of Menokeus?

KREON

When I attacked Argos,
who sent me? The metal spears went out
to bring metal from the mountains
at your request; for you know Argos
is rich in metals.

THE ELDERS

And therefore rich in spears, it seems. Some
evil things were said and we dismissed them,
        trusting you
with the reports; and we closed our ears,
fearing fear. And we shut our ears when you pulled
        the reins tighter. Just one   1070
more pull on the reins and one more battle
you said, that's all we need, but now
you are beginning to deal with us
as you deal with the enemy. How horribly
you lead your double war.

KREON

Your war!

THE ELDERS

Your war!

KREON

If I had Argos
it would be yours soon enough! Enough of this!   1080
So that rebellious girl
has stirred up all those who heard her!

THE ELDERS

Surely the sister was right to bury her brother.

KREON

Surely the commander was right to punish the
        traitor.

THE ELDERS
>The naked truth asserts its right, and right drives us
>>right to our doom.

KREON
>War makes new rights and wrongs.

THE ELDERS
>And lives by the old ones.
>War devours itself and those in need get nothing.

KREON
>Ingrates! You'll eat the meat but
>you don't like to see the cook's bloody apron! The
>>sandlewood   1090
>that I gave you to build your houses, where
>the sound of the sword is not heard, was grown in
>>Argos!
>And so far no one has sent back the bronze-plate
>that I brought you from Argos, but you huddle
>>together
>and babble about the blood-baths and complain of my
>>crassness.
>I can expect yet more provocations when the booty
>>doesn't get here.

THE ELDERS
>Man, how much longer will Thebes still be without its
>>men?

KREON
>Until your men have conquered rich Argos for you.

THE ELDERS
>Call them back, damn you, before they all die.
>Call the troops back home.

KREON
>Empty handed? Will you confirm that assignment? 1100

THE ELDERS
>Empty handed, or without hands, whatever is left of
>>flesh and blood.

KREON

> Certainly. Argos will fall, then I will call them,
> and my eldest son, Megareus, will bring them to you.
> And see to it that the doors and gates are not too
>   narrow and
> only tall enough for such as walk bent down.
> The shoulders of men of greater girth could crash the
>   palace
> door here and break the doors of the treasury there.
> And it may be there'll be such joyous embraces
> at the re-union that your hands and your arms
> shall be shaken out of their sockets. And when you
>   press with passion   1110
> against the anxious breast of their armour, mind your
>   ribs!
> Because on that happy day you'll see more bare iron
> than destitution. Many reluctant victors
> have been garlanded with chains and danced on
>   bended knees.

THE ELDERS

> Evildoer, are you threatening your own people? Are
>   you ready
> to set our own men against us?

KREON

> I want to
> discuss it with my son, Megareus.
>   (*Enter a* MESSENGER *from the battle*)

MESSENGER

> Sir, bow your head! I am a bringer
> of bad news! Stop the hasty celebration   1120
> of a victory that was announced too early! Your army
>   at Argos
> has fallen in a new battle and is in retreat.
> Your son Megareus is dead. He lies mangled
> on the hard ground of Argos. When you
> punished the retreat of Polyneikes, and the many
> in the army who opposed you were arrested
> and publicly hanged, and you yourself

hurried back to Thebes, your eldest son
immediately ordered us to advance into a new battle.
The troops had not yet slept off the bloodbath in
    their own   1130
ranks. With tired hands they raised
the battle ax still wet with Theban blood
against the men of Argos. And all too many
faces turned around toward Megareus, who,
in order to seem fiercer than the enemy,
perhaps had urged them forward in too harsh a
    voice.
And yet at first the battle's luck was with us,
for every battle rouses its own battle fever,
and blood suffices, be it ours or theirs,
and it intoxicates. What courage cannot do   1140
fear does. But weapons
and good equipment and good nourishment all play a
    part in it,
And sir, the people of Argos fought with desperation.
The women fought and the children fought.
Pots and pans, long without food,
were filled with boiling water and
poured down on us from the burned out rooftops. Even
    surviving houses
were burned down behind us, so that there were
no prepared positions in the rear to which we could
    withdraw.
Every house became a trench and every household
    article a weapon.
But still your son drove us forward and drove us
further into the city, which, devastated,
now transformed itself into a grave. Among the ruins
we were separated from one another; smoke from all
    the occupied
quarters, sheets of fire,
confounded our vision. Fleeing the fire and seeking
    the enemy,
we slew one another;
and no one knows by whose hand your son died.
The flower of Thebes. All gone.

And Thebes itself cannot last long, because   1160
the Argives are coming with men and with wagons
into our streets. And I who have seen it
am glad that it's over.
    (*He dies*)

THE ELDERS
    Woe!

KREON
    Megareus, my son!

THE ELDERS
    Don't waste time
    grieving. Gather the forces.

KREON
    Gather nothing. Down the drain.

THE ELDERS
    Drunk with the joys of victory,
    Thebes leaps up as the enemy   1170
    approaches to put her in the iron chains.
    You sold us out
    when you gave your sword away. Now
    remember your other son:
    call the younger!

KREON
    Yes, Hamon, my last one! Yes, my youngest son!
    Come help me now in my great downfall; forget
    what I said, because when I was master of many
    I could not master myself.

THE ELDERS
    Hurry to the cliffside   1180
    and remove the grave walls quickly.
    Free Antigone!

KREON
    If I let her go
    will you stand by me? You agreed
    to everything when you challenged nothing; that
        means

you're committed!

THE ELDERS
    Go!

KREON
    The ax! The ax!
        (KREON *exits*)

THE ELDERS
    Stop the dancing!
        (*Striking the cymbals*)
    Spirit of joy, who is proud of the waters   1190
    that Cadmus loved,
    come, if you want to see her again,
    your city. Travel swiftly and get here
    before nightfall, because after that
    she'll be gone.
    This, O god of joy,
    is your native city, the Bacchanalian
    Thebes, where you lived at Ismene's cold brook.
    Here you have seen the smoke of your sacrifices
            rising firmly
    above the rafters of the rooves.   1200
    But now you will not see that fire
    rise from her many houses, nor the smoke of the fire,
            nor the
    shadow of the smoke.
    For a thousand years her children saw themselves as
            masters of
    the most distant seas,
    but tomorrow they shall have, and today they have
    hardly a stone on which to lay their heads.
    In your days, god of joy,
    you sat at the cocytus with the beloved
    in the woods of Castalia. And   1210
    visited the blacksmith, smilingly
    testing the edges of the swords with your thumb.
    Often you followed the
    deathless songs of Thebes
    through the streets when they still were merry,

Oh, their weapons have mauled their own men;
their strength was consumed by exhaustion.
Oh, violence is in need of a miracle
and gentleness is in need of a little wisdom.
And now the much battered enemy stands   1220
at the gates of our palaces and commands
the bloody spears around
the seven gated mouth
and will not leave there
until our cheeks
are filled with blood.
   But here comes a girl
   pushing her way through the crowd, surely
   with news of Hamon, appointed
   by his father to lead our rescuing troops.
   (*A young woman enters as a* MESSENGER)

MESSENGER
   O wasted strength! Oh, the last sword is broken!
   Hamon is dead, bleeding by his own hand.
   I was an eye-witness; what happened earlier
   I heard from the slaves who went to their master
   on that high cliff where
   the poor corpse of Polyneikes lay, gnawed by the
     dogs.
   They washed him silently and laid him out,
   as is the custom, among fresh branches,
   and carefully built a little shelter   1240
   made of the native soil.
   Pushing past all the others the master approached
   the grave in the cliff where we women were
     standing.
   One of us heard a voice
   and loud cries from inside the chamber
   and ran to the master to tell him.
   He hurried, and as he went he was surrounded
   strangely by the dark and pitiful voices.
   Then, coming close, he called out and cried
     pathetically
   when he saw that the bolt had been torn away   1250

out of the wall, and said beseechingly, as though
he believed what he said, "That's not Hamon's
    voice.
That's not my child's voice." We obeyed our
frightened master's word; and then
we see her, Antigone, at the back of the cave among
    the graves,
hanged by the neck.
A rope made of cloth round her neck.
And there he lies—stretched out at her feet, high
    above him
bemoaning his bridal bed and the abyss below
and his father's work. And when he sees it
he goes in to him and speaks to him:
"O come out, my dear child, I beg you on my knees."
Looks at him coldly, nor answers him, staring at him,
his son confronts him
and draws his double edged sword towards him.
But when his frightened father turns
to flee, he falters. Without one more word,
standing upright, he slowly pierces the sword
into his own body. Wordless, he falls.
The dead lie with the dead. Bridal
fulfillment is found somberly in the house
of the underworld. Here comes my master himself.

THE ELDERS

The city has fallen. We were used to the law
and are lawless. Leaning on women
the defeated man comes, and
in his hands he carries a great memento
of a stupid rage...
        (Enter KREON *carrying the shirt of Hamon*)

KREON

Look at what I've got. It's the shirt. I had thought
it would have been a sword when I went to get it. My
    child died
too soon for me. Just one more battle   1280
and Argos would have surrendered! But what there
    was

of courage and of excellence was turned against me,
so now Thebes falls;
and it should fall, should fall with me, should be
    done with
and left to the vultures. That's how I want it.
    (KREON *exits with the* MAIDS)

THE ELDERS
Turned around and went
—holding nothing more in his hands than a
    bloodstained
cloth, all that was left of the house of Labdacus—
into the tottering city.
But we,
we follow him still, and
it's all downhill. Our violent
hand shall now be cut off so that it shall not strike
    again. But she
who saw it all could only help the enemy who
now comes to destroy us. For time is short
and the unknown surrounds us; and it isn't enough
just to live unthinking and happy
and patiently bear oppression
and only learn wisdom with age.